The Score-Raising Vocabulary Builder for ACT and SAT Prep & Advanced SSAT and TOEFL Study

Level 2

Paul G Simpson IV

with the Staff of Test Professors

For Rainen

The Score-Raising Vocabulary Builder for ACT and SAT Prep & Advanced SSAT and TOEFL Study

Level 2

Table of Contents

LEVEL A VOCABULARY

RELEVANT

Applicable (adjective)

The sign clearly states that the parking rules are <u>applicable</u> only on weekends and not on weekdays.

Other Common Forms: applicability (noun)

Appropriate (adjective)

When her friend questioned her about the dietary habits of the blue-footed sloth, she struggled to come up with an <u>appropriate</u> response.

Other Common Forms: appropriateness (noun)

Apt (adjective)

The teacher hailed the essay for its <u>aptness,</u> stating that it addressed the topic more clearly and directly than that of any other student.

Other Common Forms: aptness (noun)

Material (adjective)

The instructor reiterated that the only material that was <u>material</u> to the final exam was in the course textbook.

IRRELEVANT

Digressive (adjective)

The most common complaint about the teacher, who enjoyed telling personal anecdotes instead of history, was that his lectures were <u>digressive</u> and off-topic.

Other Common Forms: digression (noun)

Immaterial (adjective)

The lawyer argued that the fact that his client drove a BMW was wholly <u>immaterial</u> to the case, which involved copyright infringement.

Other Common Forms: immateriality (noun)

Incidental (adjective)

Great detective novels include seemingly <u>incidental</u> details that later prove crucial to solving the mystery.

Other Common Forms: incidentally (adverb)

Peripheral (adjective)

The fact that your cat enjoys sleeping in your shoes is quite <u>peripheral</u> to our current discussion of human anatomy.

TRUE / HONEST

Accurate (adjective)

The plot and characters of her favorite movie are not <u>accurate</u> at all, for none of the events or people actually existed in history.

Other Common Forms: accuracy (noun)

Authentic (adjective)

An <u>authentic</u> Mexican restaurant must offer dishes with jalapeno, as the pepper is a traditional ingredient in Mexican cuisine.

Other Common Forms: authenticity (noun)

Genuine (adjective)

Due to concerns about piracy, Microsoft strongly urges its customers to check for a <u>genuine</u> serial number before purchasing a new operating system.

Legitimate (adjective)

Snowboarding used to be considered merely a hobby, but it has gained <u>legitimacy</u> as a genuine sport, even gaining inclusion as an Olympic event.

Other Common Forms: legitimacy (noun)

Valid (adjective)

The doctor confirmed that my father's concern about high cholesterol was <u>valid</u> because of our family history.

Other Common Forms: validity (noun)

FALSE / LYING

Counterfeit (adjective, noun)

The <u>counterfeit</u> Louis Vuitton bags appear identical to the real ones, though they sell at only 20% of the price.

Deceitful (adjective)

Recent research, such as the fact that the average person lies to his mother once in every five interactions, suggests that <u>deceit</u> is an inescapable part of the human condition.

Other Common Forms: deceit (noun)

Fraudulent (adjective)

His insurance claims for a debilitating back injury were revealed to be <u>fraudulent</u> when he was filmed playing tackle football.

Other Common Forms: fraud (noun)

Invalid (adjective)

I was excited to receive the phone number from the beautiful girl, until I realized that the number was <u>invalid</u>, containing thirteen numbers instead of the standard ten.

Other Common Forms: invalidity (noun)

RICH / EXTRAVAGANT

Grand (adjective)

Though he had expected luxury accommodations in the five-star hotel, he was blown away by the <u>grandness</u> of his room, which included a bowling alley and a private movie theater.

Other Common Forms: grandness (noun)

Luxurious (adjective)

Dubai is renowned for its <u>luxurious</u> malls, with lobbies made of gold and fine restaurants in place of food courts.

Wealthy (adjective)

Tony never envies the <u>wealthy</u>, for he knows that money cannot buy true happiness.

Other Common Forms: wealth (noun)

RAPID REVIEW #1

Find the synonym.

1) Incidental
   (A) legitimate
   (B) deceitful
   (C) peripheral
   (D) apt

2) Applicable
   (A) digressive
   (B) luxurious
   (C) material
   (D) genuine

3) Apt
   (A) appropriate
   (B) immaterial
   (C) grand
   (D) valid

4) Fraudulent
   (A) accurate
   (B) wealthy
   (C) valid
   (D) counterfeit

5) Digressive

   (A) grand

   (B) fraudulent

   (C) immaterial

   (D) applicable

6) Luxurious

   (A) incidental

   (B) apt

   (C) invalid

   (D) grand

7) Authentic

   (A) deceitful

   (B) genuine

   (C) peripheral

   (D) immaterial

8) Material

   (A) counterfeit

   (B) digressive

   (C) legitimate

   (D) appropriate

POOR / INADEQUATE

Beggarly (adjective)

People found it hard to believe that the Silicon Valley billionaire had come from a <u>beggarly</u> background and had not owned a single computer in his childhood.

Other Common Forms: beggar (noun ✗)

Impoverished (adjective)

The dean unreasonably expects the department to achieve scientific breakthroughs, though all the labs are <u>impoverished</u> in terms of equipment.

Other Common Forms: impoverishment (noun)

Insufficient (adjective)

The detective had <u>insufficient</u> clues at hand, and thus could not proceed with the investigation.

Other Common Forms: insufficiency (noun)

Meager (adjective)

As their land provides only <u>meager</u> sustenance during the winter months, the villagers rely on stored food from the summer months in order to survive.

Other Common Forms: meagerness (noun)

GENEROUS

Beneficent (adjective)

It was <u>beneficent</u> of her uncle to lend her a car for the entire month that she visited, as it saved her time and more than a thousand dollars in rental car fees.

Other Common Forms: beneficence (noun)

benefactor (noun ☥)

Benevolent (adjective)

The local church has earned its reputation for <u>benevolence</u>, providing both food and shelter to the less fortunate.

Other Common Forms: benevolence (noun)

Bounteous (adjective)

The brochure accentuated the <u>bounteous</u> activities on the island, including fishing, diving, and snorkeling.

Other Common Forms: bounty (noun)

Hospitable (adjective)

Mr. Ismay was a very <u>hospitable</u> host who not only gave us a tour of his home but also insisted that we stay for dinner.

Other Common Forms: hospitality (noun)

GREEDY

Covetous (adjective)

Critics accused the company's CEO of <u>covetousness</u> after it was revealed that he received a multi-million dollar bonus even as the company lost money.

Other Common Forms: covetousness (noun)

Gluttonous (adjective)

In Dante's *Inferno* the third circle holds the <u>gluttonous</u>, who are guarded by the three-headed beast Cerberus.

Other Common Forms: gluttony (noun)

Miserly (adjective)

Darcy is so <u>miserly</u> that, rather than spend two dollars to have her car washed, she washes her car with buckets of water that she carries down from her apartment on the fifteenth floor.

Other Common Forms: miserliness (noun)

Stingy (adjective)

May's <u>stinginess</u> towards waitresses is not a product of her upbringing, as her father and mother always tip at least 25 percent when they dine out.

Other Common Forms: stinginess (noun)

A LOT

Abundant (adjective)

Due to <u>abundant</u> water supply and high temperatures, typhoons are common in tropical regions.

Other Common Forms: abundance (noun)

Bountiful (adjective)

The <u>bountiful</u> waters off the coast of Nantucket, which teem with fish and shellfish, have provided sustenance for untold centuries.

Other Common Forms: bounty (noun)

Incalculable (adjective)

Mark's son caused him <u>incalculable</u> pain by wrecking the family car and then getting expelled from school.

Multitude (noun)

A <u>multitude</u> of insurance policies exist, from those with a very low premium to those with a very high premium.

Other Common Forms: multitudinous (adjective)

Plentiful (adjective)

Still bearing the scars of the Great Famine of 2006, his mother always ensures that the food in the refrigerator is <u>plentiful</u>.

Other Common Forms: plenty (noun)

A LITTLE

Deficient (adjective)

Finding her knowledge of codes to be <u>deficient</u>, she researched until she felt comfortable enough to begin writing the computer program.

Other Common Forms: deficiency (noun)

Inadequate (adjective)

The two available helicopters proved <u>inadequate</u> to the task of trying to transport the more than 80 accident victims to the hospital.

Other Common Forms: inadequacy (noun)

Lack (noun, verb)

<u>Lacking</u> the required number of credits to graduate, Jeffrey must study for another year at the university.

Scarce (adjective)

El Nino brings floods to dry regions, and makes rain water <u>scarce</u> in usually humid areas.

Other Common Forms: scarcity (noun)

Shortfall (noun)

Though the city council projected a large surplus at the beginning of the year, it now admits to a <u>shortfall</u> of funding.

RAPID REVIEW #2

Find the synonym.

1) Bountiful
   (A) impoverished
   (B) abundant
   (C) beneficent
   (D) miserly

2) Meager
   (A) multitudinous
   (B) hospitable
   (C) covetous
   (D) insufficient

3) Scarce
   (A) deficient
   (B) plentiful
   (C) gluttonous
   (D) benevolent

4) Beggarly
   (A) bounteous
   (B) miserly
   (C) beneficent
   (D) impoverished

5) Multitude

   (A) scarcity

   (B) stinginess

   (C) insufficiency

   (D) abundance

6) Lack

   (A) bounty

   (B) shortfall

   (C) meagerness

   (D) glutton

7) Incalculable

   (A) hospitable

   (B) beggarly

   (C) abundant

   (D) covetous

8) Benevolent

   (A) abundant

   (B) miserly

   (C) beneficent

   (D) multitudinous

USING A LOT

Extravagant (adjective)

Even after she became wealthy, she acquired none of the <u>extravagance</u> of her peers, who lived in mansions and drove luxury cars.

Other Common Forms: extravagance (noun)

Immoderate (adjective)

Economists warned that, if the government continued its <u>immoderate</u> spending, the country would soon face bankruptcy.

Lavish (adjective, verb)

The <u>lavishness</u> of the chocolate dessert, which was topped with 14k gold flakes, ensured that it was the most expensive dessert in the city.

Other Common Forms: lavishness (noun)

Unreasonable (adjective)

After James spent more than two thousand dollars on Pokémon cards, his parents again warned him to curb his <u>unreasonable</u> spending habits.

USING A LITTLE

Conserve (verb)

In order to <u>conserve</u> the town's water resources, the mayor temporarily banned all lawn-watering and car-washing.

Other Common Forms: conservation (noun)

Economical (adjective)

Her decision to stop eating fast food is not only healthy but also <u>economical</u>, as food prepared at home is cheaper.

Other Common Forms: economy (noun)

Sparing (adjective)

Because the coach was <u>sparing</u> in her criticism, players paid greater attention when she did challenge them.

Temperate (adjective)

He consciously maintained <u>temperate</u> television viewing habits, ensuring that he never watched more than one hour each day.

Other Common Forms: temperance (noun)

LARGE

Astronomical (adjective)

The odds against winning the lottery are so <u>astronomical</u> that one has a better chance of dying before the drawing occurs than of winning the jackpot.

Colossal (adjective)

The Loch Ness monster is commonly described as a <u>colossal</u> dinosaur with shark fins and an extremely long neck.

Other Common Forms: colossus (noun)

Massive (adjective)

The bottle clearly states that, if the chemical touches your skin, you should immediately rinse with a <u>massive</u> amount of water.

Other Common Forms: mass (noun)

Monstrous (adjective)

With the help of adrenaline, Rachel summoned a <u>monstrous</u> amount of strength to carry the piano out of the burning apartment.

SMALL

Microscopic (adjective)

Steven is highly interested in examining sea water at a
microscopic level, particularly the different types of plankton.

Miniature (adjective)

Leonard was surprised when his time machine arrived because he
had assumed it was a miniature replica and not a full-size one that
he could sit in.

Other Common Forms: miniaturized (adjective)

Negligible (adjective)

The radiation emitted by cell phones is so negligible that it does
not pose any threat to the health of users.

Tiny (adjective)

When Robin went out with the surgeon, she joked that she had
"TB," or tiny bladder.

MAKE LARGE / SWELL

Balloon (verb)

Interest in the trial <u>ballooned</u> after the national media began to focus on the case.

Enhance (verb)

The parenting classes have greatly <u>enhanced</u> Jacob's parenting skills, making him a much better father.

Other Common Forms: enhancement (noun)

Expand (verb)

Scientists hypothesize that the sun will eventually <u>expand</u> to a size so large that it will swallow all the planets in the solar system.

Other Common Forms: expansion (noun)

Inflate (verb)

After he realized that the air in his tires was low, he pulled into a gas station in order to <u>inflate</u> his tires to the proper pressure.

Other Common Forms: inflation (noun)

RAPID REVIEW #3

Find the synonym.

1) Extravagant
   (A) colossal
   (B) negligible
   (C) economical
   (D) lavish

2) Astronomical
   (A) sparing
   (B) microscopic
   (C) massive
   (D) temperate

3) Balloon
   (A) lavish
   (B) inflate
   (C) conserve
   (D) lack

4) Immoderate
   (A) monstrous
   (B) miniature
   (C) economical
   (D) unreasonable

5) Enhancement

   (A) conservation

   (B) extravagance

   (C) colossus

   (D) expansion

6) Massive

   (A) miniaturized

   (B) immoderate

   (C) colossal

   (D) negligible

7) Sparing

   (A) lavish

   (B) temperate

   (C) astronomical

   (D) massive

8) Lavishness

   (A) extravagance

   (B) conservation

   (C) mass

   (D) inflation

MAKE SMALL

Compress (verb)

It's easier to send a batch of pictures when they are <u>compressed</u> into a single file; otherwise, they are too large to be sent in a timely fashion.

Other Common Forms: compressed (adjective)

Condense (verb)

As the period did not allow enough time for the entire movie, the teacher <u>condensed</u> it into a short, 30-minute clip that featured the most important scenes.

Other Common Forms: condensed (adjective)

Decline (verb, noun)

Because Tony's stamina is in <u>decline</u>, he can no longer run in the New York City Marathon.

Shrink (verb)

When she opened the dryer, Cindy was surprised to find her jeans <u>shrunken</u>, now two sizes too small.

Other Common Forms: shrunken (adjective)

SHORT-LIVED

Impermanent (adjective)

An alternative to tattoos, henna designs are <u>impermanent</u> and usually disappear after approximately one week.

Other Common Forms: impermanence (noun)

Momentary (adjective)

The traffic accident caused only a <u>momentary</u> delay in traffic, with cars moving freely after only a brief time.

Other Common Forms: moment (noun)

Passing (adjective)

The controversy was <u>passing and soon</u> faded from the collective memory of the town.

Temporary (adjective)

Due to the renovation of the airport, the first and second boarding gates are <u>temporarily</u> closed.

Other Common Forms: temporarily (adverb)

LONG-LIVED

Ceaseless (adjective)

My ceaseless complaints finally succeeded in convincing the school to install hand dryers in order to reduce paper waste.

Eternal (adjective)

A valentine's gift such as chocolate is temporary and easily forgotten, while a gift such as a diamond is meant to be eternal and never forgotten.

Other Common Forms: eternity (noun)

Immortal (adjective)

Immortality has always been the hope of many who would rather live forever than deal with death.

Other Common Forms: immortality (noun)

Lasting (adjective)

In contrast to its predecessor, this new deodorant is much more lasting, effective for up to twelve hours.

Permanent (adjective)

The data stored in RAM is temporary and disappears when the computer is turned off, whereas the data stored on the hard drive is permanent unless it is deleted by the user.

Other Common Forms: permanence (noun)

HUMBLE

Meek (adjective)

H.W. Todd once remarked that <u>meekness</u> should never be mistaken for fear, as the truly humble are the most courageous among us.

Other Common Forms: meekness (noun)

Modest (adjective)

While a pompous athlete takes all the credit for himself, a <u>modest</u> athlete attributes his success to his coach and teammates.

Other Common Forms: modesty (noun)

Unpretentious (adjective)

Despite rumors to the contrary, the actress proved herself to be down-to-earth in a series of frank and <u>unpretentious</u> interviews.

ARROGANT

Conceited (adjective)

The heroes of Greek mythology are often <u>conceited</u>, full of themselves and their accomplishments, a character flaw that often leads to their downfall.

Other Common Forms: conceit (noun)

Condescending (adjective)

Despite his wealth and global fame, James is never <u>condescending</u> towards others, earning a reputation as one of the most humble men in Hollywood.

Other Common Forms: condescension (noun)

Pretentious (adjective)

While truly interested in the subject of astrobiology, Luke could not stand the <u>pretentiousness</u> of the professor, who always seemed more interested in making herself seem smart than in teaching the knowledge to others.

Other Common Forms: pretentiousness (noun)

Vain (adjective)

Roxanne is known for her <u>vanity</u> among her friends, who always joke about her habit of checking herself out in a mirror every few moments .

Other Common Forms: vanity (noun)

LEVEL A REVIEW

Find the synonym.

1) Ceaseless
   (A) inadequate
   (B) legitimate
   (C) immoderate
   ✓ (D) immortal

2) Multitudinous
   (A) colossal
   ✓ (B) abundant
   (C) lasting
   (D) vain

3) Extravagant
   ✓ (A) astronomical
   (B) immoderate
   (C) ceaseless
   (D) scarce

4) Balloon
   (A) lack
   (B) compress
   (C) conserve
   ✓ (D) expand

37

5) Conceited

   (A) momentary

✓(B) beggarly

   (C) vain

   (D) modest

6) Appropriate

   (A) insufficient

   (B) passing

   (C) economical

✓(D) material

7) Fraudulent

✓(A) counterfeit

   (B) temperate

   (C) miniature

   (D) immaterial

8) Authentic

   (A) incidental

   (B) fraudulent

✓(C) genuine

   (D) benevolent

9) Microscopic

(A) extravagant

(B) conceited

(C) pretentious

✓ (D) miniature

10) Colossal

(A) digressive

✓ (B) astronomical

(C) apt

(D) plentiful

11) Temperate

(A) bountiful

(B) sparing

(C) luxurious

✓ (D) beneficent

12) Condense

(A) balloon

(B) lavish

✓ (C) compress

(D) conserve

13) Momentary

   (A) passing
   (B) meek
   (C) unreasonable
   (D) negligible

14) Grand

   (A) tiny
   (B) accurate
   (C) luxurious
   (D) material

15) Benevolent

   (A) appropriate
   (B) insufficient
   (C) authentic
   (D) beneficent

16) Bounty

   (A) counterfeit
   (B) immortality
   (C) plenty
   (D) impoverishment

17) Stinginess

(A) validity

(B) miserliness

(C) deficiency

(D) vanity

18) Meagerness

(A) modesty

(B) authenticity

(C) hospitality

(D) insufficiency

19) Pretentious

(A) massive

(B) condescending

(C) permanent

(D) extravagant

20) Shortfall

(A) legitimacy

(B) lack

(C) aptness

(D) gluttony

LEVEL B VOCABULARY

RELEVANT

Apropos (adjective)

Rather than provide an <u>apropos</u> answer to the moderator's question, the politician instead offered a rambling, off-topic message.

Cogent (adjective)

The <u>cogency</u> of the lawyer's argument convinced the judges, who ruled to uphold the Miranda laws.

Other Common Forms: cogency (noun)

Pertinent (adjective)

When deciding on a job offer, commute time is a <u>pertinent</u> factor that needs to be taken into account.

Other Common Forms: pertinence (noun)

.

IRRELEVANT

Inapposite (adjective)

As the two films share nothing at all in common, your comparison of them is extremely <u>inapposite</u>.

Marginal (adjective)

The fact that he was listening to music is <u>marginal</u> to the car accident, since the music played no role in the crash.

Other Common Forms: marginality (noun)

Rambling (adjective)

When nervous or confused, the teacher has a tendency to <u>ramble</u> on instead of deliver cogent lectures.

Other Common Forms: ramble (verb)

Tangential (adjective)

What you are saying right now is completely <u>tangential</u> to the main themes of the book.

Other Common Forms: tangent (noun)

TRUE / HONEST

Candid (adjective)

The new captain prefers <u>candid</u> communication to flattery, so he welcomes all constructive criticisms of his leadership.

Candor (noun)

At a recent fundraiser, the state representative insulted the audience with his <u>candor</u>, remarking that he was only present for the money and not because he enjoyed the event.

Forthright (adjective)

Small children are renowned for their <u>forthrightness,</u> saying exactly what they think without regard to social niceties.

Other Common Forms: forthrightness (noun)

Frank (adjective)

Sometimes it is better to be <u>frank</u> with people, as lying only complicates matters in the future.

Other Common Forms: frankness (noun)

FALSE / LYING

Apocryphal (adjective)

Though often accepted as true, many stories of George Washington's childhood are <u>apocryphal</u> legends.

Disingenuous (adjective)

Rather than insult his appearance, she provided a <u>disingenuous</u> response that masked her hatred of his neon-green jean shorts.

Other Common Forms: disingenuousness (noun)

Fictive (adjective)

The suspect insisted that she was innocent and that police accounts of her actions were <u>fictive</u> inventions.

Prevaricate (verb)

The penalty of perjury can be invoked if a person <u>prevaricates</u> in their testimony, which requires them to swear an oath of honesty.

Other Common Forms: prevarication (noun)

RICH / EXTRAVAGANT

Affluent (adjective)

Most ancient cultures expressed a preference for chubbier women because weight was a symbol of <u>affluence</u>.

Other Common Forms: affluence (noun)

Lavish (adjective, verb)

The <u>lavishness</u> of the 52-room mansion belied the fact that its owner was actually bankrupt.

Other Common Forms: lavishness (noun)

Prosperous (adjective)

Because the emperor was too bellicose and spent too much money on war, the dynasty was <u>prosperous</u> for only a decade.

Other Common Forms: prosperity (noun)

RAPID REVIEW #5

Find the synonym.

1) Apropos

   (A) fictive

   (B) frank

   (C) tangential

   (D) pertinent

2) Frank

   (A) rambling

   (B) candid

   (C) apocryphal

   (D) affluent

3) Affluent

   (A) cogent

   (B) prosperous

   (C) marginal

   (D) candid

4) Inapposite

   (A) disingenuous

   (B) forthright

   (C) tangential

   (D) apropos

5) Fictive

   (A) rambling

   (B) apocryphal

   (C) lavish

   (D) prosperous

6) Forthrightness

   (A) cogency

   (B) prosperity

   (C) affluence

   (D) candor

7) Disingenuousness

   (A) candor

   (B) prevarication

   (C) pertinence

   (D) tangent

8) Marginal

   (A) prosperous

   (B) cogent

   (C) frank

   (D) tangential

POOR / INADEQUATE

Barren (adjective)

Unlike the Fertile Crescent in Asia Minor, which holds abundant water and rich soil, the Sahara Desert is <u>barren</u>.

Other Common Forms: barrenness (noun)

Destitute (adjective)

Approximately half the world's total population is functionally <u>destitute</u>, living on less than one U.S. dollar per day.

Other Common Forms: destitution (noun)

Pauper (noun ⚥)

When the economy of a country declines, more people are unemployed and the number of <u>paupers</u> rises.

GENEROUS

Altruistic (adjective)

Some argue that performing an act of true <u>altruism</u>, in which there is no personal benefit, is exceedingly difficult, if not impossible.

Other Common Forms: altruism (noun)

Liberal (adjective)

The family demonstrated its <u>liberality</u> by welcoming the stranger into its home and providing for his every need.

Other Common Forms: liberality (noun)

Open-handed (adjective)

Warren Buffet has earned kudos for his <u>openhandedness</u>, particularly after his recent charitable donation of 37 billion dollars.

Other Common Forms: openhandedness (noun)

Philanthropic (adjective)

Most museums rely on <u>philanthropy</u> to survive, as income from admission tickets almost always falls short of operating expenses.

Other Common Forms: philanthropist (noun ⚲)

philanthropy (noun)

GREEDY

Acquisitive (adjective)

The company gained a reputation for <u>acquisitiveness</u> after it bought more than 200 companies in just two years.

Other Common Forms: acquisitiveness (noun)

acquisition (noun)

Close-fisted (adjective)

His reluctance to donate in public might lead you to judge him as <u>close-fisted</u>; in reality, he simply prefers to practice altruism anonymously.

Insatiable (adjective)

Around the world pigs are characterized by their <u>insatiable</u> appetite, which drives them to eat anything at any time.

Other Common Forms: insatiability (noun)

Ravenous (adjective)

Upon returning home after two years of working abroad in Hong Kong, Susan was <u>ravenous</u> for her mother's cooking.

A LOT

Ample (adjective)

Despite <u>ample</u> evidence of its harms, cigarette smoking continues to be practiced throughout the world.

Copious (adjective)

The doctor instructed the flu patient, who was in danger of dehydration, to drink <u>copious</u> amounts of water.

Other Common Forms: copiousness (noun)

Plenteous (adjective)

IIis reasons for moving to California are <u>plenteous</u>; they include better job opportunities, cheaper housing, and more temperate weather.

Other Common Forms: plentiful (adjective)

plenty (noun)

Profuse (adjective)

To the surprise of scientists, the formerly barren area surrounding the Chernobyl nuclear plant now hosts a <u>profusion</u> of wildlife.

Other Common Forms: profusion (noun)

A LITTLE

Depleted (adjective)

Though he felt <u>depleted</u>, completely devoid of strength and energy, the marathoner somehow managed to cover the final five miles of the race.

Other Common Forms: depletion (noun)

Scanty (adjective)

The judge deemed the presented evidence too <u>scanty</u>, lacking in any depth or substance, and promptly dismissed the case.

Other Common Forms: scantiness (noun)

Wanting (adjective)

David found the entire film <u>wanting</u>, as it lacked a coherent script and competent acting.

Other Common Forms: want (noun, verb)

RAPID REVIEW #6

Find the synonym.

1) Copious
   (A) liberal
   ✓(B) profuse
   (C) destitute
   (D) depleted

2) Ravenous
   (A) scanty
   ✓(B) insatiable
   (C) profuse
   (D) philanthropic

3) Depleted
   (A) close-fisted
   (B) plenteous
   ✓(C) scanty
   (D) insatiable

4) Plenty
   (A) acquisitiveness
   (B) want
   ✓(C) profusion
   (D) philanthropist

5) Openhandedness

   (A) insatiability

   (B) depletion

   (C) copiousness

 ✓(D) liberality

6) Destitution

 ✓(A) barrenness

   (B) liberality

   (C) scantiness

   (D) profusion

7) Ample

   (A) open-handed

✓ (B) plenteous

   (C) ravenous

   (D) depleted

8) Altruism

   (A) pauper

   (B) copiousness

   (C) acquisition

 ✓(D) philanthropy

USING A LOT

Exorbitant (adjective)

Apartment rental fees in Los Angeles are expensive, but not anywhere near as <u>exorbitant</u> as in New York, where the average rent is more than three times as expensive.

Other Common Forms: exorbitance (noun)

Inordinate (adjective)

Critics of the U.S. political system argue that the current costs of presidential campaigns are <u>inordinate</u>, with each party spending hundreds of millions of dollars per campaign cycle.

Intemperate (adjective)

Bill Gates, fearful of <u>intemperance</u> on the part of his children, has stated that he will limit each of their inheritances to ten million dollars, a miniscule fraction of his expected legacy.

Other Common Forms: intemperance (noun)

Undue (adjective)

Arguing that homework places an <u>undue</u> burden on already overwhelmed high school students, some critics have advocated a dramatic reduction of, if not an outright ban on, homework.

USING A LITTLE

Abstinent (adjective)

Aristotle argued not for <u>abstinence</u> in one's life but for moderation, a balance that, he contended, ensures happiness.

Other Common Forms: abstinence (noun)

Austere (adjective)

Facing unexpected budget shortfalls, the township adopted <u>austerity</u> measures, including water usage restrictions and reductions in the budgets of the police and fire departments.

Other Common Forms: austerity (noun)

Frugal (adjective)

Although generally modest, Rose was vain about her <u>frugality</u>, frequently bragging about the ways in which she recycled old objects instead of purchasing new ones.

Other Common Forms: frugality (noun)

Stinting (adjective)

The vacationing couple suspected that the hotel was <u>stinting</u> when they discovered that their room did not contain toiletries, a television, or even a bed.

LARGE

Corpulent (adjective)

The cat's increasing <u>corpulence</u> alarmed the veterinarian, who advocated a diet that would, she hoped, help the cat lose twenty pounds.

Other Common Forms: corpulence (noun)

Immense (adjective)

The <u>immensity</u> of some cruise ships can be understood only when aboard, where they appear large even in the vastness of the ocean.

Other Common Forms: immensity (noun)

Mammoth (adjective)

The <u>mammoth</u> art installation took a volunteer crew of 2,000 more than three weeks to complete.

Vast (adjective)

Christopher Columbus greatly underestimated the <u>vastness</u> of the distance between Spain and India; his expedition was already running low on supplies when it reached the Caribbean.

Other Common Forms: vastness (noun)

SMALL

Diminutive (adjective)

Lured by the cuteness and <u>diminutive</u> size of baby pigs, some people adopt them as pets, only to be overwhelmed when the pigs reach their mature size.

Other Common Forms: diminution (noun)

Miniscule (adjective)

While the individual value of a United States penny is <u>miniscule,</u> the collective value of these pennies is more than twenty billion dollars.

Petite (adjective)

Though they expect a small stature, those who meet horse-racing jockeys often are shocked by just how <u>petite</u> they really are.

Trifling (adjective)

Car sales people often lure customers into large purchases with <u>trifling</u> extras such as a free oil change or a free key chain.

Other Common Forms: trifle (noun)

MAKE LARGE / SWELL

Amplify (verb)

During mating season, male right whales <u>amplify</u> their calls so that they can reach across several thousand square miles.

Other Common Forms: amplification (noun)

Augment (verb)

She <u>augmented</u> her music collection every Friday after she received her paycheck, often downloading and purchasing dozens of songs.

Other Common Forms: augmentation (noun)

Magnify (verb)

While attempting to better the school's chronic absence problem, the new zero-tolerance policy only <u>magnified</u> the issue by punishing those with legitimate excuses for absence.

Other Common Forms: magnification (noun)

Protract (verb)

The negotiations, expected to last but a few weeks, have become <u>protracted</u> to the point that no one expects them to conclude for at least another two years.

Other Common Forms: protracted (adjective)

RAPID REVIEW #7

Find the synonym.

1) Trifling
   (A) abstinent
   (B) miniscule
   (C) protracted
   (D) inordinate

2) Austere
   (A) magnified
   (B) petite
   (C) intemperate
   (D) frugal

3) Magnified
   (A) amplified
   (B) exorbitant
   (C) corpulent
   (D) frugal

4) Intemperance
   (A) abstinence
   (B) immensity
   (C) exorbitance
   (D) trifle

5) Mammoth

 (A) stinting

 (B) austere

 (C) immense

 (D) diminutive

6) Frugality

 (A) vastness

 (B) augmentation

 (C) amplification

 (D) austerity

7) Undue

 (A) inordinate

 (B) protracted

 (C) mammoth

 (D) austere

8) Miniscule

 (A) vast

 (B) diminutive

 (C) exorbitant

 (D) stinting

MAKE SMALL

Collapse (verb, noun)

The economy's extended <u>collapse</u> has ensured the loss of 25 percent of all the country's jobs.

Constrict (verb)

Recent construction has left only two lanes of the six-lane highway open, <u>constricting</u> traffic so much that three-hour delays are common.

Other Common Forms: constricted (adjective)

Contract (verb)

Cramps are the common term for a <u>contracted</u> muscles that remain <u>contracted</u>, causing the sufferer severe pain.

Other Common Forms: contracted (adjective)

Deflate (verb)

The car tire <u>deflated</u> imperceptibly over time, until it was almost completely empty and in need of more air.

Other Common Forms: deflated (adjective)

SHORT-LIVED

Ephemeral (adjective)

Though all life is <u>ephemeral</u>, that of a fruit fly is particularly fleeting as it lasts only a few days.

Other Common Forms: ephemerality (noun)

Fleeting (adjective)

The plane crash survivors watched the <u>fleeting</u> light of the emergency flare arc across the sky, each hoping that it could be seen from afar.

Other Common Forms: fleetingness (noun)

Transient (adjective)

The tropics are marked by <u>transient</u> storms, which unleash torrential downpours that are quickly replaced by intense sunshine.

Other Common Forms: transience (noun)

LONG-LIVED

Durable (adjective)

Consumer goods, such as refrigerators and washing machines, once made to be <u>durable</u> are now made to break down in a short time, a practice known as "planned obsolescence."

Other Common Forms: durability (noun)

Enduring (adjective)

The pyramids of Egypt were meant to be <u>enduring</u>, indestructible testaments to those entombed within them.

Imperishable (adjective)

By successfully manipulating the genes of the mice, the scientists have made them virtually <u>imperishable</u> because the mice do not age.

Perpetual (adjective)

Most agree that a <u>perpetual</u> motion machine is impossible to create because forces such as friction will always cause motion to stop.

Persistent (adjective)

To become an Olympic athlete requires <u>persistence</u>, intensive focus and training that lasts not years but decades.

Other Common Forms: persistence (noun)

HUMBLE

Unassuming (adjective)

The <u>unassuming</u> police detective refused to take credit for the arrest, and subsequent conviction, of the criminal, instead honoring her colleagues for all of their hard work.

Unobtrusive (adjective)

The student was so <u>unobtrusive</u> that, even after a year at the school, no one seemed to know his name, not even the teachers.

Other Common Forms: unobtrusiveness (noun)

ARROGANT

Aloof (adjective)

The doctor's reputation for aloofness was accentuated when he posted a sign on his office door that read "The world's greatest thoracic surgeon—living or dead."

Egoistic (adjective)

Countless popular magazines attest to the fact that egoism among movie stars is not only accepted but encouraged.

Other Common Forms: egoism (noun)

Haughty (adjective)

Though the football fan had no experience, he haughtily asserted that he could do a better job than any professional on the team.

Other Common Forms: haughtiness (noun)

Patronizing (adjective)

The worst professors are those who give simplistic and patronizing lectures because they do not believe that students could possible understand their respective specialties.

Other Common Forms: patronize (verb)

Pompous (adjective)

Jerry is unassuming and engaging in conversation, quite the opposite of what one would expect after reading his books, which adopt a distant and pompous tone.

LEVEL B REVIEW

Find the synonym.

1) Plenteous

   (A) barren

   (B) apropos

   (C) profuse

   (D) liberal

2) Augmented

   (A) open-handed

   (B) immense

   (C) fictive

   (D) amplified

3) Haughty

   (A) pertinent

   (B) contracted

   (C) deflated

   (D) pompous

4) Persistent

   (A) enduring

   (B) trifling

   (C) austere

   (D) ample

5) Petite

   (A) depleted

   (B) altruistic

   (C) diminutive

   (D) mammoth

6) Austere

   (A) insatiable

   (B) frugal

   (C) petite

   (D) trenchant

7) Apropos

   (A) ephemeral

   (B) intemperate

   (C) pertinent

   (D) undue

8) Destitute

   (A) exorbitant

   (B) cogent

   (C) miniscule

   (D) barren

9) Insatiable

  (A) fleeting

  (B) unobtrusive

  (C) ravenous

  (D) imperishable

10) Fictive

  (A) perpetual

  (B) copious

  (C) frank

  (D) apocryphal

11) Tangential

  (A) candid

  (B) inapposite

  (C) wanting

  (D) scanty

12) Ample

  (A) barren

  (B) unassuming

  (C) copious

  (D) durable

13) Intemperate

   (A) sparing

   (B) profuse

   (C) exorbitant

   (D) frugal

14) Mammoth

   (A) stinting

   (B) immense

   (C) lavish

   (D) affluent

15) Perpetual

   (A) imperishable

   (B) marginal

   (C) forthright

   (D) open-handed

16) Trifling

   (A) philanthropic

   (B) miniscule

   (C) rambling

   (D) abstinent

17) Contract

(A) prevaricate

(B) patronize

(C) ramble

(D) constrict

18) Unobtrusive

(A) corpulent

(B) diminutive

(C) unassuming

(D) disingenuous

19) Scanty

(A) wanting

(B) apocryphal

(C) vast

(D) ravenous

20) Ephemeral

(A) acquisitive

(B) inapposite

(C) transient

(D) austere

LEVEL C VOCABULARY

RELEVANT

Apposite (adjective)

While fascinating, her tales of travel in the Sahara were not <u>apposite</u> to the baseball forum; therefore the moderator deleted all of her posts.

Germane (adjective)

When he could not add anything <u>germane</u> to a conversation, he preferred to remain silent rather than make inapposite remarks.

Trenchant (adjective)

The reporter's <u>trenchant</u> accounts of life in New York City gained her a wide readership and several prestigious prizes.

Other Common Forms: trenchancy (noun)

IRRELEVANT

Discursive (adjective)

After posting his short story online, James was dismayed that all of the comments were <u>discursive</u> and did not address the story in any form.

Other Common Forms: discursiveness (noun)

Excursive (adjective)

He lawyer employed a strategy of excursiveness, attempting to confuse the jury with as much <u>immaterial</u> information as possible.

Other Common Forms: excursiveness (noun)

Extraneous (adjective)

Critics have argued that the increasing mobility and power of devices such as cell phones have made it harder for the average person to filter out <u>extraneous</u> information and to focus on important tasks.

Other Common Forms: extraneousness (noun)

TRUE / HONEST

Fidelity (noun)

Dogs are renowned for their <u>fidelity</u>, remaining true to their masters no matter the circumstances.

Incontrovertible (adjective)

In science the one <u>incontrovertible</u> truth is that no theory is <u>incontrovertible</u>; new evidence can disprove a theory at any time.

Other Common Forms: incontrovertibility (noun)

Indubitable (adjective)

Her ATM receipt, which showed a balance of negative thirty dollars, revealed the <u>indubitable</u> truth of her poverty.

Other Common Forms: indubitably (adverb)

Veracious (adjective)

The <u>veracity</u> of all the business reporter's articles was called into question after it was discovered that, in his latest story, he had invented quotes from imaginary people.

Other Common Forms: veracity (noun)

FALSE / LYING

Fabricate (verb)

He insisted upon the veracity of the outlandish story, stating that he did not have enough imagination to <u>fabricate</u> such a wild tale.

Other Common Forms: fabrication (noun)

Fallacious (adjective)

When her colleagues demonstrated the <u>fallaciousness</u> of her argument, she was forced to extensively rewrite the paper.

Other Common Forms: fallaciousness (noun)

Specious (adjective)

Many potential voters are disaffected by the <u>specious</u> debates of partisan politics.

Other Common Forms: speciousness (noun)

Spurious (adjective)

Oprah became furious when she learned of <u>spurious</u>, fictional details in the book, which had been marketed as a true memoir.

Other Common Forms: spuriousness (noun)

RICH / EXTRAVAGANT

Opulent (adjective)

Ancient reports attest to the <u>opulence</u> of the imperial court, whose very floors were made of gold and encrusted with diamonds.

Other Common Forms: opulence (noun)

Profuse (adjective)

She became quickly embarrassed by the <u>profuse</u> praise heaped upon her by the host, particularly as she did not believe herself to be the world's greatest singer, songwriter, and dancer.

Other Common Forms: profusion (noun)

Remunerative (adjective)

Though he possessed a passion for philosophy, he finally acquiesced to his parents' demand that he study business in preparation for a more <u>remunerative</u> profession.

Other Common Forms: remuneration (noun)

RAPID REVIEW #9

Find the synonym.

1) Fallacious

   (A) apposite

   (B) indubitable

   (C) opulent

   (D) spurious

2) Indubitable

   (A) remunerative

   (B) spurious

   (C) excursive

   (D) incontrovertible

3) Apposite

   (A) profuse

   (B) germane

   (C) veracious

   (D) extraneous

4) Excursive

   (A) trenchant

   (B) opulent

   (C) extraneous

   (D) specious

5) Trenchant

   (A) remunerative

   (B) apposite

   (C) incontrovertible

   (D) excursive

6) Discursive

   (A) profuse

   (B) fallacious

   (C) excursive

   (D) indubitable

7) Fabrication

   (A) opulence

   (B) spuriousness

   (C) fidelity

   (D) discursiveness

8) Veracity

   (A) profusion

   (B) incontrovertibility

   (C) speciousness

   (D) trenchancy

POOR / INADEQUATE

Indigent (adjective, noun ⚥)

The true rate of <u>indigence</u> is underreported, because the impoverished move more frequently and are harder to track.

Other Common Forms: indigence (noun)

Insolvent (adjective)

Rather than admit his company's <u>insolvency</u>, the now-imprisoned owner forged loan documents in a desperate attempt to mask the bankruptcy.

Other Common Forms: insolvency (noun)

Penurious (adjective)

Her parents, though <u>penurious</u> throughout her childhood, always made sure that she was properly fed, clothed, and educated.

Other Common Forms: penuriousness (noun)

GENEROUS

Largess (noun)

Despite her wealth, she was never respected in the community, for her <u>largess</u> extended only to herself and to her pet beagles.

Magnanimous (adjective)

The philanthropist's reputation for <u>magnanimity</u> was strengthened by his latest donation of 100 million dollars to the local school district.

Other Common Forms: magnanimity (noun)

Munificent (adjective)

The stranger was astounded by the <u>munificence</u> of the townspeople, who ensured that he was well-fed and housed during his two-week stay.

Other Common Forms: munificence (noun)

GREEDY

Avaricious (adjective)

After not eating for three days, he scanned the food in the refrigerator with <u>avaricious</u> eyes.

Other Common Forms: avarice (noun)

Rapacious (adjective)

In the Middle Ages, the Vikings earned their reputation for <u>rapacity</u> by systematically stealing all valuables from those whom they conquered.

Other Common Forms: rapacity (noun)

Ravenous (adjective)

Hyenas are <u>ravenous</u> scavengers that scour forests and fields in search of abandoned carcasses.

Voracious (adjective)

He possessed a <u>voracious</u> appetite for vintage cars, eventually amassing a collection of more than seven hundred.

Other Common Forms: voraciousness (noun)

A LOT

Cornucopia (noun)

Early explorers depicted the land as a <u>cornucopia</u> of riches that dripped with gold, silver, and pearls.

Myriad (adjective)

Life on Earth is so <u>myriad</u> that scientists can not accurately estimate the number of species that call it home.

Plethora (noun)

A <u>plethora</u> of customer complaints eventually drove the poorly-managed company out of business.

Surfeit (noun)

Inflation is not caused by a lack of available currency, but rather by a <u>surfeit</u> of it.

Voluminous (adjective)

<u>Voluminous</u> reports of an impending attack, broadcast incessantly on radio and television, fueled panic among the country's citizens.

A LITTLE

Dearth (noun)

Tourists in New York City rightly complain about the <u>dearth</u> of public restrooms, which are nearly impossible to find.

Paucity (noun)

They shut down the website not due to a <u>paucity</u> of funds but rather due to a lack of visitors.

Privation (noun)

Raised in an upper-class family, she was ill-prepared for the <u>privation</u> that she witnessed in the slums of Manila.

RAPID REVIEW #10

Find the synonym.

1) Indigent

(A) munificent

(B) avaricious

(C) penurious

(D) myriad

2) Dearth

(A) voraciousness

(B) largess

(C) cornucopia

(D) paucity

3) Plethora

(A) privation

(B) surfeit

(C) magnanimity

(D) insolvency

4) Rapacity

(A) avarice

(B) munificence

(C) paucity

(D) surfeit

5) Voluminous

   ✓ (A) myriad

    (B) penurious

    (C) ravenous

    (D) magnanimous

6) Insolvent

    (A) avaricious

    (B) munificent

    (C) indigent

    (D) rapacious

7) Munificence

    (A) dearth

    (B) avarice

    (C) privation

   ✓ (D) magnanimity

8) Ravenous

    (A) voluminous

   ✓ (B) voracious

    (C) munificent

    (D) myriad

USING A LOT

Prodigal (adjective)

Often spending more than a million dollars a week on lavish parties, Seager gained notoriety for his <u>prodigality</u>.

Other Common Forms: prodigality (noun)

Profligate (adjective, noun ☧)

After winning the multi-million dollar jackpot, she descended into a <u>profligate</u> lifestyle that quickly left her bankrupt.

Other Common Forms: profligacy (noun)

Spendthrift (adjective, noun ☧)

Despite warnings to save for retirement, many Americans continue to be <u>spendthrifts</u> who spend as much as, or more than, they earn.

Unstinting (adjective)

He was <u>unstinting</u> towards his prized pet Chihuahuas, purchasing for them only the finest food, clothing, and accessories.

USING A LITTLE

Abstemious (adjective)

She remained <u>abstemious</u> in speech, entering the conversation only in extremely rare circumstances.

Other Common Forms: abstemiousness (noun)

Ascetic (adjective, noun ☥)

Living without electricity or running water, the <u>ascetic</u> adopted a lifestyle that few others in his country would be able to stomach.

Parsimonious (adjective)

Her <u>parsimony</u> over the years allowed her to save enough money to pay for the college education of her three children.

Other Common Forms: parsimony (noun)

Provident (adjective)

The hibernation of grizzly bears allows them to burn as few calories as possible, a <u>provident</u> behavior that ensures survival.

Other Common Forms: providence (noun)

Spartan (adjective)

Against the advice of her doctor, she began a <u>spartan</u> diet that consisted only of water, bread, and bananas.

LARGE

Capacious (adjective)

The children attending the circus were dumbfounded by the capaciousness of the clown car, which ultimately fit more than a dozen clowns and seven large dogs.

Other Common Forms: capaciousness (noun)

Commodious (adjective)

Cramped into a minute seat in economy class, he could only dream of the commodious accommodations in first class.

Other Common Forms: commodiousness (noun)

Gargantuan (adjective)

Measuring up to 100 feet and weighing upwards of 200 tons, the blue whale is the most gargantuan creature known to have lived on Earth.

Prodigious (adjective)

She showcased her prodigious knowledge of trivia by winning 138 consecutive games of Trivial Pursuit against her friends.

SMALL

Infinitesimal (adjective)

She could never understand people who littered, since it takes but <u>infinitesimal</u> amounts of time and energy to properly dispose of trash.

Minute (adjective)

The manufacture of any computer requires hundreds of <u>minute</u> measurements that ensure that all of the parts will function correctly.

Other Common Forms: minuteness (noun)

Paltry (adjective)

In return for the release of the hostages, the kidnapper demanded the surprisingly <u>paltry</u> sum of forty-two dollars..

Other Common Forms: paltriness (noun)

MAKE LARGE / SWELL

Accrue (verb)

In the period before hibernation, the brown bear <u>accrues</u> weight quickly, gaining as much as thirty pounds per week.

Other Common Forms: accrued (adjective)

Distend (verb)

Chronic malnutrition is often marked by a <u>distended</u> abdomen, a symptom that causes the stomach to appear disproportionately large.

Other Common Forms: distended (adjective)

Tumesce (verb)

Because several diseases can cause <u>tumescence</u> of the fingers, the doctors are not yet sure which of them the patient possesses.

Other Common Forms: tumescent (adjective)

tumescence (noun)

Wax (verb)

As the military draft continued, the ranks of the army <u>waxed</u> until it reached an unprecedented size.

Other Common Forms: waxing (adjective)

RAPID REVIEW #11

Find the synonym.

1) Profligate

   (A) parsimonious

   (B) gargantuan

   (C) prodigal

   (D) paltry

2) Abstemious

   (A) infinitesimal

   (B) spartan

   (C) accrued

   (D) unstinting

3) Infinitesimal

   (A) minute

   (B) spendthrift

   (C) distended

   (D) provident

4) Tumescent

   (A) ascetic

   (B) minute

   (C) distended

   (D) capacious

5) Prodigious

   (A) waxing

   (B) gargantuan

   (C) paltry

   (D) commodious

6) Capacious

   (A) profligate

   (B) spartan

   (C) abstemious

   (D) commodious

7) Ascetic

   (A) prodigal

   (B) infinitesimal

   (C) parsimonious

   (D) unstinting

8) Spendthrift

   (A) provident

   (B) minute

   (C) unstinting

   (D) ascetic

MAKE SMALL

Abbreviate (verb)

Due to the typhoon, the schools ran an <u>abbreviated</u> schedule that allowed students to leave early.

Other Common Forms: abbreviated (adjective)

Abridge (verb)

In lieu of full versions of feature films, the country's citizens always see edited, <u>abridged</u> versions that meet the government's regulations.

Other Common Forms: abridged (adjective)

Curtail (verb)

When her grades began to suffer, she <u>curtailed</u> her extracurricular activities, which had taken up more than thirty hours per week.

Other Common Forms: curtailed (adjective)

Truncate (verb)

In order to facilitate understanding and convenience, journal articles are prefaced by a <u>truncated</u> version of the findings.

Other Common Forms: truncated (adjective)

Wane (verb)

In order to block out excessive light, cats' pupils <u>wane</u> on extremely bright and sunny days.

Other Common Forms: waning (adjective)

SHORT-LIVED

Evanescent (adjective)

It's very difficult to capture a perfect picture of an <u>evanescent</u> lightning strike, as it occurs in the matter of milliseconds.

Other Common Forms: evanescence (noun)

Fugacious (adjective)

The existence of a may fly is a <u>fugacious</u> one, lasting from just thirty minutes to one day.

Other Common Forms: fugaciousness (noun)

Transitory (adjective)

Their love was <u>transitory</u>, ending as soon as class finished its day-long field trip to the Natural History Museum.

LONG-LIVED

Abiding (adjective)

A visit to the zoo as a child sparked in her an <u>abiding</u> passion for birds, ultimately leading her to become one of the country's foremost ornithologists.

Incessant (adjective)

The children's <u>incessant</u> complaints about the planned vacation led the parents to finally decide to take the trip themselves and to leave the children at home.

Unceasing (adjective)

Those with chronic arthritis suffer <u>unceasing</u> pain, which can be lessened, but not eliminated, by medication.

Unremitting (adjective)

The city remains unconquered thus far, despite <u>unremitting</u> attacks that have endured for more than two decades.

HUMBLE

Menial (adjective)

Because he overcame menial origins to become the president of the country, he disliked more <u>pompous</u> members of his government.

Retiring (adjective)

His friends knew that he was a <u>retiring</u> type who preferred not to talk about himself but about others.

ARROGANT

Impudent (adjective)

She accused the waiter of <u>impudence</u> because, rather than smile and greet them politely, he sneered at them in an improper fashion.

Other Common Forms: impudence (noun)

Insolent (adjective)

The <u>insolence</u> of his actions, which involved him marching in to the boss' office and rudely demanding a promotion, led to his immediate dismissal.

Other Common Forms: insolence (noun)

Supercilious (adjective)

When he refused to talk to reporters or sign autographs for fans, the baseball player quickly earned a reputation for <u>superciliousness</u>.

Other Common Forms: superciliousness (noun)

Swaggering (adjective)

In the wake of the multi-million dollar deal, she praised only herself and ignored the assistance of her dozen team members as she <u>swaggered</u> past their desks.

Other Common Forms: swagger (verb, noun)

LEVEL C REVIEW

Find the synonym.

1) Penurious

    (A) apposite

    (B) extraneous

    (C) capacious

    (D) indigent

2) Impudent

    (A) germane

    (B) menial

    (C) insolent

    (D) truncated

3) Abstemious

    (A) prodigious

    (B) profligate

    (C) parsimonious

    (D) paltry

4) Voracious

    (A) supercilious

    (B) insolvent

    (C) ravenous

    (D) voluminous

5) Fabrication

   (A) parsimony

   (B) dearth

   (C) fallaciousness

   (D) commodiousness

6) Minute

   (A) infinitesimal

   (B) distended

   (C) myriad

   (D) swaggering

7) Menial

   (A) curtailed

   (B) germane

   (C) incontrovertible

   (D) retiring

8) Provident

   (A) opulent

   (B) retiring

   (C) fugacious

   (D) ascetic

9) Incessant

  (A) unremitting

  (B) abiding

  (C) transitory

  (D) abstemious

10) Tumesce

  (A) fabricate

  (B) abridge

  (C) wane

  (D) distend

11) Rapacious

  (A) indigent

  (B) germane

  (C) avaricious

  (D) veracious

12) Myriad

  (A) transitory

  (B) insolent

  (C) voluminous

  (D) infinitesimal

13) Curtail

 (A) tumesce

 (B) truncate

 (C) distend

 (D) accrue

14) Supercilious

 (A) voracious

 (B) penurious

 (C) unremitting

 (D) swaggering

15) Dearth

 (A) munificence

 (B) surfeit

 (C) paucity

 (D) fidelity

16) Magnanimous

 (A) munificent

 (B) opulent

 (C) impudent

 (D) paltry

17) Abridge

(A) wax

(B) fabricate

(C) abbreviate

(D) distend

18) Abiding

(A) minute

(B) unceasing

(C) evanescent

(D) unstinting

19) Extraneous

(A) incessant

(B) incontrovertible

(C) excursive

(D) fugacious

20) Surfeit

(A) spendthrift

(B) cornucopia

(C) impudence

(D) excursiveness

Answer Keys

Rapid Review 1

1) C
2) C
3) A
4) D
5) C
6) D
7) B
8) D

Rapid Review 2

1) B
2) D
3) A
4) D
5) D
6) B
7) C
8) C

Rapid Review 3

1) D
2) C
3) B
4) D
5) D
6) C
7) B
8) A

Level A Review

1) D
2) B
3) B
4) D
5) C
6) D
7) A
8) C
9) D
10) B
11) B
12) C
13) A
14) C
15) D
16) C
17) B
18) D
19) B
20) B

Rapid Review 5

1) D
2) B
3) B
4) C
5) B
6) D
7) B
8) D

Rapid Review 6

1) B
2) B
3) C
4) C
5) D
6) A
7) B
8) D

Rapid Review 7

1) B
2) D
3) A
4) C
5) C
6) D
7) A
8) B

Level B Review

1) C
2) D
3) D
4) A
5) C
6) B
7) C
8) D
9) C
10) D
11) B
12) C
13) C
14) B
15) A

16) B
17) D
18) C
19) A
20) C

Rapid Review 9

1) D
2) D
3) B
4) C
5) B
6) C
7) B
8) B

Rapid Review 10

1) C
2) D
3) B
4) A
5) A
6) C
7) D
8) B

Rapid Review 11

1) C
2) B
3) A
4) C
5) B
6) D
7) C
8) C

Level C Review

1) D
2) C
3) C
4) C
5) C
6) A
7) D
8) D
9) A
10) D
11) D
12) C
13) B
14) D
15) C
16) A
17) C
18) B
19) C
20) B

QUICK LISTS

Relevant

applicable	appropriate	apt	material
apropos	cogent	pertinent	
apposite	germane	trenchant	

Irrelevant

digressive	immaterial	incidental	peripheral
inapposite	marginal	rambling	tangential
discursive	excursive	extraneous	

True / Honest

accurate	authentic	genuine	legitimate	valid
candid	candor	forthright	frank	
fidelity	incontrovertible		indubitable	
veracious				

False / Lying

counterfeit	deceitful	fraudulent	invalid
apocryphal	disingenuous	fictive	prevaricate
fabricate	fallacious	specious	spurious

Rich / Extravagant

grand	luxurious	wealthy
affluent	lavish	prosperous
opulent	profuse	remunerative

Poor / Inadequate

beggarly	impoverished	insufficient	meager
barren	destitute	pauper	
indigent	insolvent	penurious	

Generous

beneficent	benevolent	bounteous	hospitable
altruistic	liberal	open-handed	philanthropic
largess	magnanimous		munificent

Greedy

covetous	gluttonous	miserly	stingy
acquisitive	close-fisted	insatiable	ravenous
avaricious	rapacious	ravenous	voracious

A Lot

abundant	bountiful	incalculable	multitude
ample	copious	plenteous	profuse
cornucopia	myriad	plethora	surfeit
voluminous			

A Little

deficient	inadequate	lack	scarce
depleted	scanty	wanting	
dearth	paucity	privation	

Using a Lot

extravagant	immoderate	lavish	unreasonable
exorbitant	inordinate	intemperate	undue
prodigal	profligate	spendthrift	unstinting

Using a Little

conserve	economical	sparing	temperate
abstinent	austere	frugal	stinting
abstemious	ascetic	parsimonious	provident	spartan

Large

astronomical	colossal	massive	monstrous
corpulent	immense	mammoth	vast
capacious	commodious	gargantuan	prodigious

Small

microscopic	miniature	negligible	tiny
diminutive	miniscule	petite	trifling
infinitesimal	minute	paltry	

Make Large / Swell

balloon	enhance	expand	inflate
amplify	augment	magnify	protract
accrue	distend	tumesce	wax

Make Small

compress	condense	decline	shrink
collapse	constrict	contract	deflate
abbreviate	abridge	curtail	truncate
wane			

Short-Lived

impermanent	momentary	passing	temporary
ephemeral	fleeting	transient	
evanescent	fugacious	transitory	

Long-Lived

ceaseless	eternal	immortal	lasting
durable	enduring	imperishable	perpetual
persistent	abiding	incessant	unceasing
unremitting			

Humble

meek	modest	unpretentious
unassuming	unobtrusive	
menial	retiring	

Arrogant

conceited	condescending	pretentious	vain	
aloof	egoistic	haughty	patronizing	
pompous	impudent	insolent	supercilious	swaggering

OTHER TITLES FROM FUSION PRESS

SAT Practice Test (Kindle Edition)

5 SAT Math Practice Tests

5 SAT Critical Reading Practice Tests

5 SAT Writing Practice Tests

10 SAT Vocabulary Practice Tests

5 Fantastically Hard SAT Math Practice Tests

5 Fantastically Hard SAT Critical Reading Practice Tests

5 Fantastically Hard SAT Writing Practice Tests

10 Fantastically Hard SAT Vocabulary Practice Tests

5 PSAT Math Practice Tests

5 PSAT Writing Practice Tests

10 PSAT Vocabulary Practice Tests

5 Fantastically Hard PSAT Math Practice Tests

5 Fantastically Hard PSAT Critical Reading Practice Tests

5 Fantastically Hard PSAT Writing Practice Tests

10 Fantastically Hard PSAT Vocabulary Practice Tests

Score-Raising Vocabulary Builder for ACT and SAT (Level 1)

Score-Raising Vocabulary Builder for ACT and SAT (Level 3)

Score-Raising Vocabulary Builder for ACT and SAT (Level 4)

Score-Raising Vocabulary Builder for GRE and GMAT (Level 1)

Score-Raising Vocabulary Builder for GRE and GMAT (Level 2)

Score-Raising Vocabulary Builder for GRE and GMAT (Level 3)

Score-Raising Vocabulary Builder for GRE and GMAT (Level 4)